Best of Friends 6
The yearbook of Creative Monochrome

Editor
Roger Maile

BEST OF FRIENDS 6
The yearbook of Creative Monochrome
Editor: ROGER MAILE
Editorial assistant: Alex Dilley
Image scanning: Nicholas Charlton

Published in the UK by Creative Monochrome Ltd
Courtney House, 62 Jarvis Road, South Croydon, CR2 6HU

British Library Cataloguing-in-Publication Data:
A catalogue record for this book is available from the British Library.

ISBN 1 873319 35 5
First edition, 1999

ISSN 1359-446X

Printed in England by Alderson Brothers Printers Ltd,
Columbian House, Pool Road, West Molesey, Surrey, KT8 2NZ.

Introduction

In virtually every field of creative human endeavour, the 9:1 ratio between perspiration and inspiration seems to prevail. The images in this book may be (I hope, will be) inspiring, but their production depends on that subtle mix of hard work with technical and craft skills to bring creative inspiration to fruition. Take away the effort and expertise, and the inspiration will be wasted. There are some who believe their work has transcended technical excellence, but their images do not usually support such a bold assertion – sloppy work, however inspired, remains sloppy work.

For most monochrome workers, the creative process extends from the planning and conception of the image to the execution and presentation of the print. I have always felt that having control from start to finish is one of the attractions of monochrome work, and I find it odd that so many professionals are content that their part of the exercise is completed once the shutter release has been pressed. To leave one's film processing and print-making to a surrogate seems such an indifferent form of creative parenthood. Although there is no requirement for self-processing in submissions for Best of Friends, I doubt that any of the selected prints have been made by anyone other than the photographer.

One only has to see the large number of prints which fail at the early stages of selection for the book, to appreciate the importance of the 'perspiration' element. Whilst some do fail through lack of any apparent inspiration (or by failing to match wavelengths with the subjective preferences of the selector), many images with real potential have been let down by inadequate craft skills. Most often the problems appear to have started with exposure and film development – there is much to be said for Barry Thornton's adage that you cannot make a fine print from a coarse negative. I know that some regard this is as a far too restrictive philosophy, but generally those who adopt a salvage approach to print-making are more likely to produce superficial effects than meaningful images.

But for all the technical expertise and craft skills, the absolutely essential ingredient is the eye for the image. Using the word 'creative' in our business name sometimes seems something of a millstone, because it is too often associated with trickery. But the act of creating a photographic image is essentially one of selection: choosing the subject matter, selecting what is shown and what is concealed, arranging the elements within the picture, deciding the angle of view and selecting that fraction of a second in which all these elements are brought together and captured on film.

My objective as the selector of this collection of images is to find those captured moments which best illustrate the potential of this exciting medium. The criteria for selection are varied: some are chosen for their originality and freshness of approach, some for their emotional impact, others for their ability to convey a message or because they capture the spirit of their subject, some for their dramatic impact or for the sheer beauty of the work. I have tried to select work which reflects a broad range of subject matter and photographic styles.

So what is the purpose of bringing all these images together in book form? Firstly, it stems from the simple belief that photographs are made to be seen, rather than stuffed away in bottom drawers and albums. For many photographers, there is little opportunity to have their work seen by more than a handful of people: through the medium of this book, they can be shared with thousands. Although this can also be achieved by magazine publication or by inclusion on a web-site, the nature of the book is a more permanent record. Secondly, I believe that seeing the work of fellow labourers in the field of photography can be truly inspiring: not in terms of imitation, but as a means of showing the possibilities of photography and encouraging one to renewed personal effort and creative endeavour.

However, there is only space in a book such as this for a limited number of images and that inevitably means that some aspirations will have been dented during the selection process. I know from the correspondence received how frustrating and hurtful this can be, but I also know the sense of achievement of those who have overcome such setbacks and have eventually been successful in getting images selected. It is satisfying that several photographers have attributed personal progress in their image-making to both the inspiration of the work selected and the incentive of aiming for publication. I hope that, in this way, Best of Friends will remain a powerful force for encouraging excellence in monochrome photography.

The Friends groups

Creative Monochrome exists to promote the art of monochrome photography. It is deliberately a broad church, encouraging all styles of work and diverse subject matter. We act as a forum for the exchange of information and as a medium for sharing images and thoughts on image-making. These objectives are achieved through the Friends of Creative Monochrome – a group of over 5,000 people with a shared passion for black and white photography.

There are two forms of subscription to the Friends of Creative Monochrome. The Mono subscription brings Friends our bi-monthly magazine, 10% discount on purchases from our mail order catalogue, and entitlement to participate in the Best of Friends 'competition'. The subscription is £7.50 per year in Europe or £12.50 outside Europe. The Best of Friends subscription offers the same benefits and, additionally, a copy of the Best of Friends yearbook and calendar and a saving of £6 on each entry for Best of Friends. This subscription costs £30 in Europe and £40 elsewhere.

Digital Friends is a relatively new group for those interested in digital imaging. The subscription includes the bi-monthly full colour *Digital Photo Art* magazine and a range of special offers and discounts on digital materials and equipment. The subscription is £20 per year in the UK, £25 in the rest of Europe and £30 elsewhere.

To subscribe, contact Creative Monochrome Ltd, Courtney House, 62 Jarvis Road, South Croydon, Surrey CR2 6HU (tel: 020 8686 3282; fax: 020 8681 0662; e-mail: roger@cremono.demon.co.uk).

Best of Friends Awards

Each year we ask Friends, their partners and other readers to vote for their favourite images in the book. These votes decide who wins the BoF Awards medals and which images will appear in the Best of Friends calendar for the following year. There are 12 medals: two gold, four silver and six bronze.

Anyone who has had the chance to view the images in the book is entitled to vote. Each person has 10 votes to allocate. You can give one vote to each of 10 prints, or all 10 votes to one print, or any combination in between (for example, 4, 3, 2, 1). The only restrictions are that votes must be allocated in whole numbers and that a photographer may not vote for his or her own photographs.

To vote, for each image selected, write down the plate number (not the page number), the name of the photographer and the number of votes awarded. As a small incentive to participate, we will pick six entries out of the hat in a prize draw for books from the Creative Monochrome Contemporary Portfolio series, so you also need to include your name and address on the voting sheet.

Send your votes to Creative Monochrome Ltd, Courtney House, 62 Jarvis Road, South Croydon, Surrey, CR2 6HU to arrive no later than 31 March 2000. Alternatively, you can vote by fax (020 8681 0662) or by e-mail: roger @cremono.demon.co.uk.

The prints on this page are previous medal winners and are not eligible for these Awards.

Award winners from Best of Friends 5:
(from the top)
No title, *Kevin Bridgwood (gold)*
Thirlmere, *Alfred Hoole (silver)*
Black Mount, Rannoch Moor II,
Paul Wheeler (silver)

Award winners from Best of Friends 5:
(from the top)
Highway, *Roy Rainford (gold)*
Kerry, *Gerry Coe (silver)*
Appleby Fair II, *Marshall Calvert (silver)*

Index of contributors

(The numbers shown are the plate numbers rather than the page numbers.)

Portfolio

1
Lych gate, St Barnabas
Alan Thompson

2
Basilique Ste-Madeline, Vézelay, France
Duncan Unsworth

3
Interior of St Ouen, Rouen, France (during cleaning)
James Austin

(top left) 4 **Clan McGregor Mausoleum**, *Jim Bennett*
(bottom left) 5 **Redundant**, *Roy Lewis*
(above) 6 **The old priory**, *Peter Rees*

(top left) 7 **Lake District #3**, *Göran Stenberg*
(bottom left) 8 **Cottage of the woods**, *Sue Durant*
(above) 9 **Pisa Duomo, Italy, from the Tower**, *James Austin*

(left) 10 **Pemaquid Point lighthouse**, *Carolyn Bross*
(above) 9 **Slains Castle, Scotland**, *Graham Lowe*

12
Booth, Luddenden Dean
Kirk Toft

13
Binibeca #6
Joseph George

(top) 14 **Victorian pumping station**, *Ann Miles*
(bottom) 15 **Iron works, Shropshire**, *Ann Miles*
(right) 16 **Untitled**, *Peter Motton*

(top left) 17 **Storage tank, Dundee**, *Malcolm Thomson*
(bottom left) 18 **Sky sculpture #5**, *Alan Brown (Staffs)*
(above) 19 **Swimmer**, *Simon Welch*

(left) 20 **Light pattern**, *Mel Ridgers*
(above) 21 **Agricultural lines II**, *Brian Harvey*

22
Sky sculpture #7
Alan Brown (Staffs)

23
Sky sculpture #6
Alan Brown (Staffs)

(top left) 24 **Cafeteria**, *Bob Stevenson*
(bottom left) 25 **Occasional table**, *Peter Waters*
(above) 26 **For in that sleep**, *John Clow*

(*above*) 27 **Hairfall**, *Trevor Legate*
(*right*) 28 **Beyond the fringe**, *Ray Anderson*

28

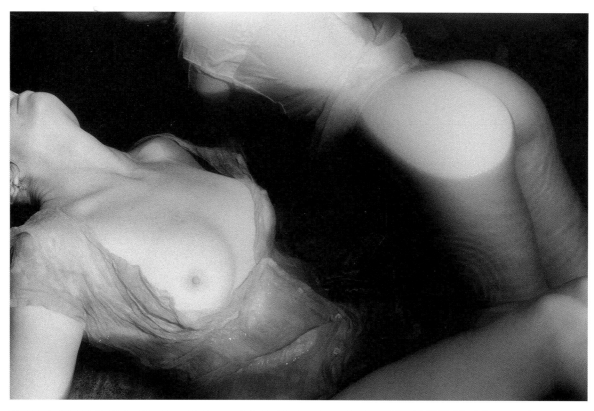

(top) 29 **Floating**, *Shirlie Phillips*
(bottom) 30 **Untitled**, *Roy Elwood*

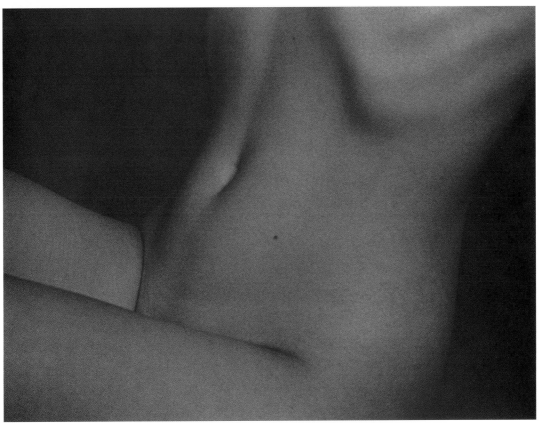

(*above*) 31 **Floating woman**, *Carolyn Bross*
(*right*) 32 **Nude 1**, *Andrew Foley*

(top left) 33 **Contours**, *Ron Abrahams*
(bottom left) 34 **At the window**, *Gary Phillips*
(above) 35 **Sonya**, *Edward Gordon*

33

36
The window
Brian Ebbage

37
Typical woodland clearing
Trevor Legate

38
Pennywort wall
Anne Newell

39
Basket of Inula
Sue Davies

(left) 40 **Tulips**, *John Reed*
(right) 41 **Tulip #2**, *Nigel Jarvis*

(left) 42 **Tulip #1**, *Nigel Jarvis*
(right) 43 **Tulips**, *Jim Bennett*

44
Iceland poppy buds
John Reed

45
Image of nature #3
David Miller (Tyne & Wear)

46
Sprouting barley
Filmer Lee

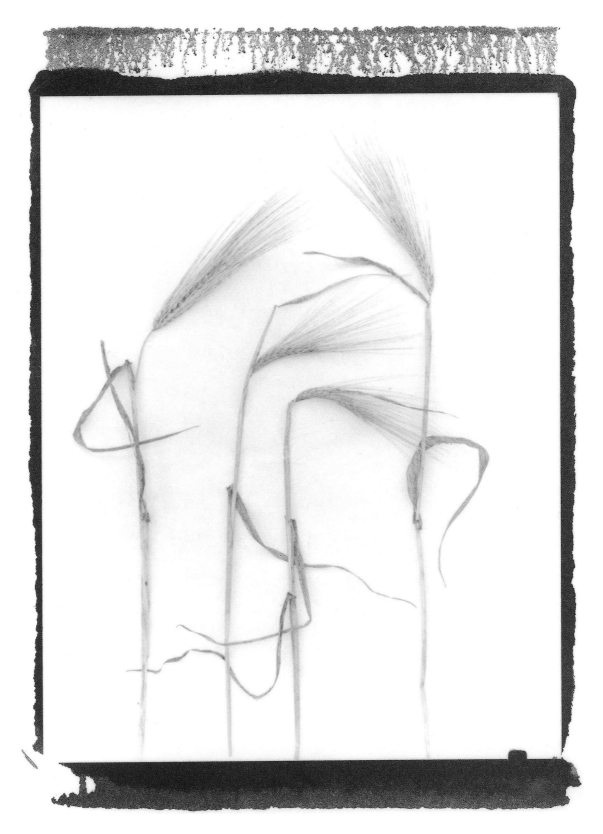

47
Barley
Filmer Lee

48
Black wall, Durness
Simon Denison

49
White horse in the sky
Alan Thompson

(*left*) 50 **Buachaille Etive Mor**, *Derek Singleton*
(*above*) 51 **Deserted croft, Skye**, *Derek Singleton*

(top) 52 **Hodge Close**, *Tom Richardson*
(bottom) 53 **Agra Moor, West Yorkshire**, *Alfred Hoole*

(top) 54 **Fingal Valley**, *Michael Calder*
(bottom) 55 **Windblown**, *Gary Phillips*

(top left) 56 **Glyder Fawr I**, *Tom Dodd*
(bottom left) 57 **Glyder Fawr II**, *Tom Dodd*
(above) 58 **Snow at Lech, Austria**, *Hazel Sanderson*

51

59
Loch Duartmore, Sutherland
John Fenn

60
Untitled
Rod Thornbury

(top left) 61 **After the storm**, *Gerry Coe*
(bottom left) 62 **Haweswater**, *Derek Singleton*
(above) 63 **Mam Tor, Peak District**, *Duncan Unsworth*

(above) 64 **Resting place**, *Peter Clark*
(top right) 65 **Roots**, *Kathleen Harcom*
(bottom right) 66 **Snowdrops**, *Michael Cant*

67
Harmony
Kathleen Harcom

68
Tree of life
Richard Ross

69
Hawthorn at Gaswell
Gareth Rees-Roberts

70
Frith Wood
Gareth Rees-Roberts

(top left) 71 **Last sunlight**, *Arnold Hubbard*
(bottom left) 72 **Frosty frieze**, *Arnold Hubbard*
(above) 73 **First snow of winter**, *Alfred Hoole*

74
Beacon Hill
Don Maslen

75
West Blean Wood
Trevor Crone

(top) 76 **Mountain oak**, *Richard Clegg*
(bottom) 77 **Woodland detail**, *Kevin Bridgwood*

66

(top) 78 **Fingal Valley morning**, *Michael Calder*
(bottom) 79 **Defiance**, *Alan Brown (Staffs)*

(left) 80 **My little Roman**, *Lisa Thompson*
(above) 81 **Family**, *Scarlet James*

82
Brittany
Eleanor Brown

83
Felicity
Gerry Coe

84
Natalina
Scarlet James

85
Sean
Roger Maile

(top left) 86 **Jo-Anne**, *Andrew Gibson*
(bottom left) 87 **Lemmy**, *Andrew Foley*
(above) 88 **Passive**, *Ian Mellor*

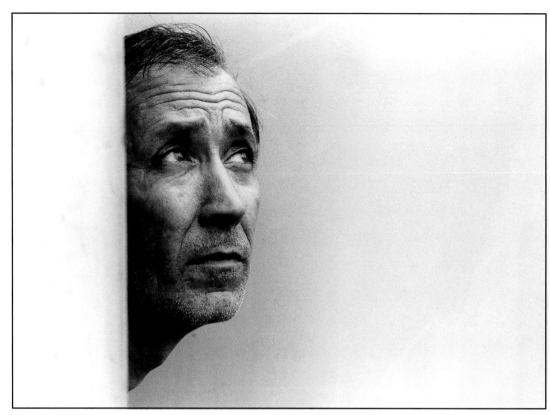

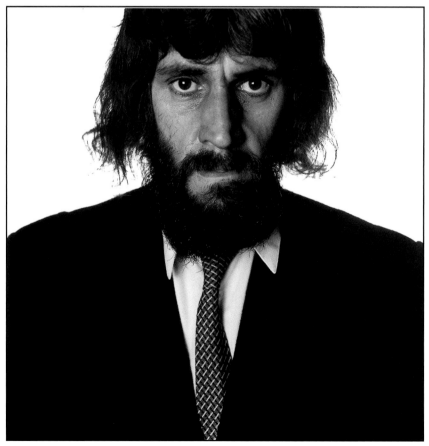

(top left) 89 **Emergence**, *Gary Phillips*
(bottom left) 90 **Duke**, *Andrew Foley*
(above) 91 **Howard, our window cleaner**, *Trevor Fry*

(top left) 92 **The vicar**, *Barbie Lindsay*
(bottom left) 93 **The look**, *Roger Ford*
(above) 94 **Sorting fares**, *Kevin Bridgwood*

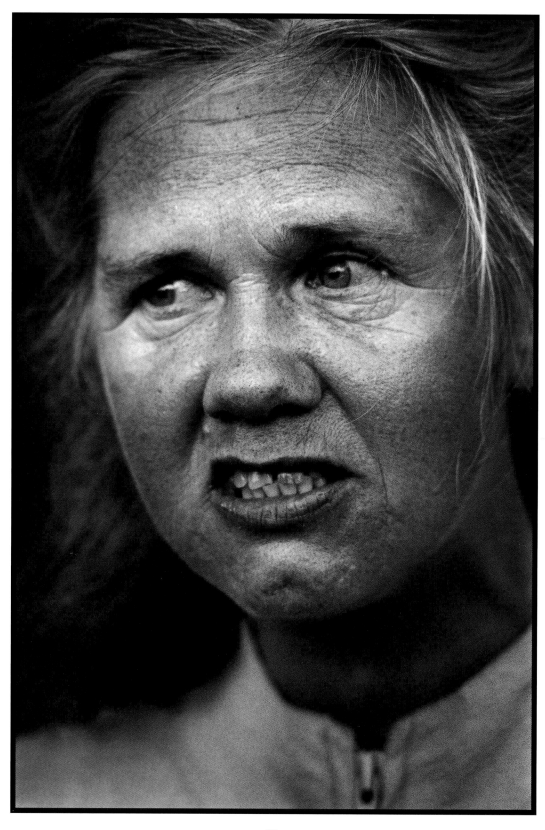

95
Untitled
Edward Gordon

96
Untitled (Oleobrom process)
Kirk Toft

97
Knut
Signe Drevsjø

98
Soldier boy
Garry Corbett

(top) 99 **Beetle of Britain**, *Roy Lewis*
(bottom) 100 **A moment in time, Gateshead**, *Trevor Ermel*

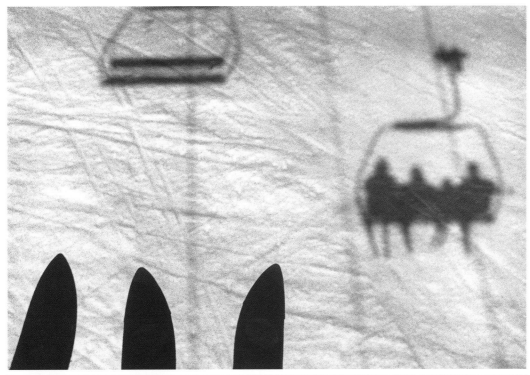

(top) 101 **In the Alps**, *Nick Stout*
(bottom) 102 **Elevador da Gloria, Lisbon, Portugal**, *Johannes Müller*

(above) 103 **Rialto Bridge, 1 January 1998**, *Brian Taylor*
(right) 104 **Gondolas**, *Arthur Smith*

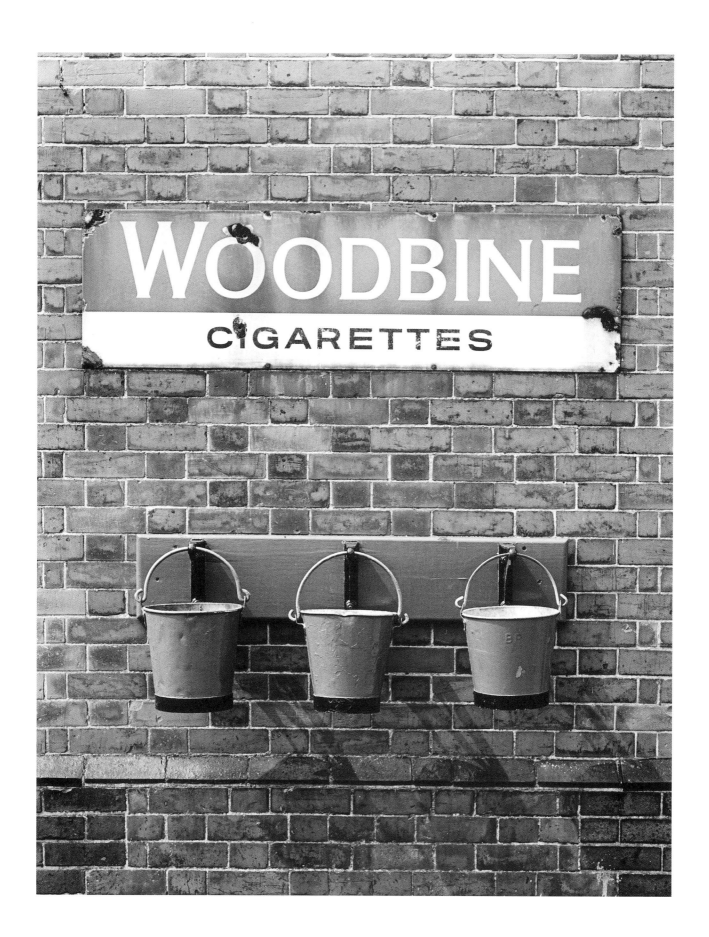

(left) 105 **In case of fire**, *D Thurlow*
(above) 106 **Gêm Cardiau**, *O Tudur Owen*

107
Minha Gente
Carlos de Fazio

108
They think it's all over
Alan Brown (Tyne & Wear)

Niels Peter Jensen
27·5
1859
13·6
1918

(above) 109 **Coastal grave**, *Len Perkis*
(top right) 110 **The Ten Commandments Stone**, *Emma Weal*
(bottom right) 111 **Impression and relief**, *Mike Kielecher*

(top) 112 **Please no cars**, *Gill Terry*
(bottom) 113 **Forward looking**, *John Devenport*

(top) 114 **Signpost, two crosses**, *Simon Denison*
(bottom) 115 **Pennine Way**, *Brian Harvey*

(left) 116 **Untitled**, *Neil Bedwell*
(above) 117 **The steps**, *Anne Newell*

118
Untitled
Neil Bedwell

119
Board walk
Neil Souch

(above) 120 **Twitcher**, *Chris Holt*
(top right) 121 **The chase**, *Ann Miles*
(bottom right) 122 **Untitled**, *Lesley Aggar*

123
Stockade
Paul Damen

124
Catfield Hall barn, Norfolk
Mark Oakland

(above) 125 **Indian Tawny Eagle**, *David Askew*
(right) 126 **European Eagle Owl**, *David Askew*

(above) 127 **Turkey grace,** *Daniel Acevedo*
(top right) 128 **The eye of the Highland,** *Keith Urro*
(bottom right) 129 **The happy pig,** *Pauline Rook*

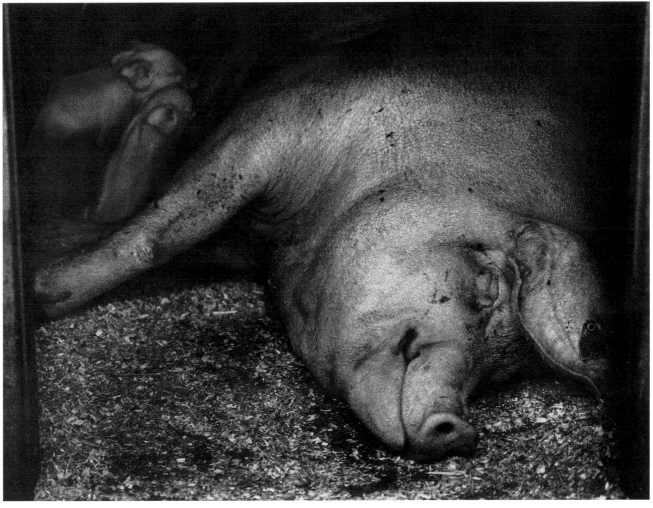

(top left) 130 **Same horse**, *Keith Urro*
(bottom left) 131 **Rider of the storm**, *Shirlie Phillips*
(top) 132 **Shop!**, *Len Perkis*
(bottom) 133 **Ram**, *Keith Urro*

(above) 134 **They're off!**, *Hilary Fairclough*
(top right) 135 **Olga defects to West!**, *Glyn Edmunds*
(bottom right) 136 **A dog's life**, *Hilary Fairclough*

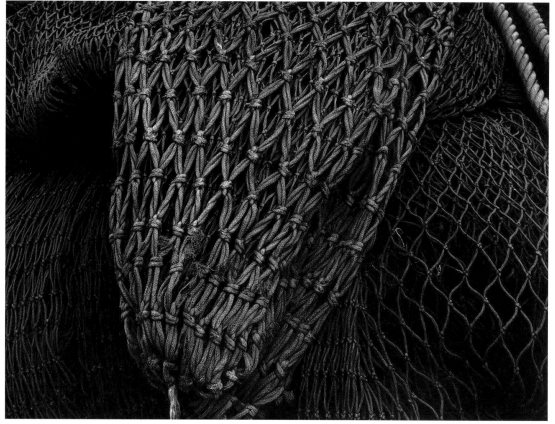

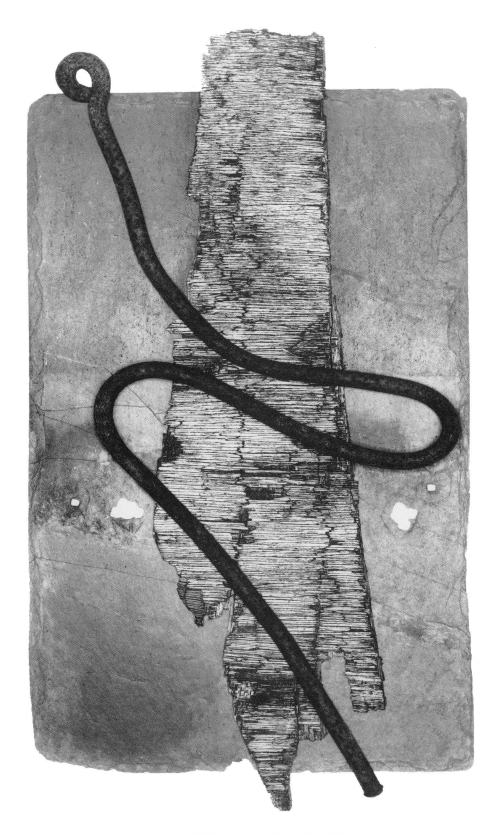

(top left) 137 **Study in white**, *Fred Hunt*
(bottom left) 138 **Nets**, *R Williams*
(above) 139 **Three forms**, *Andrew Sanderson*

113

140
Mémoires du temps – horaire – 09
Jean-Jacques Lucas

141
Mémoires du temps – horaire – 04
Jean-Jacques Lucas

142
Sand pattern #1
Steve Terry

143
Mémoires du temps – horaire – 10
Jean-Jacques Lucas

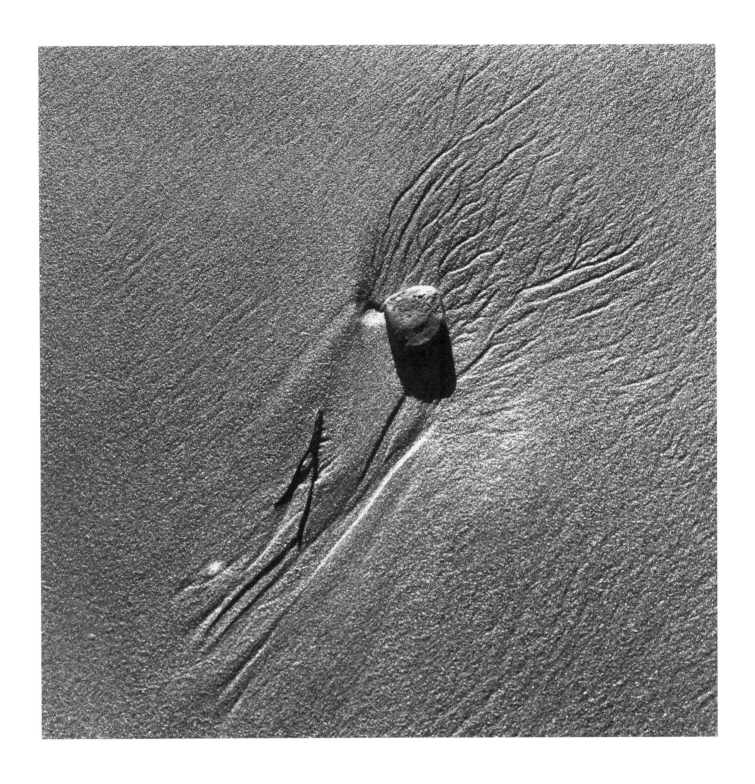

144
Grit
Jim Shipp

145
The racetrack, Death Valley
Peter Clark

146
Rock series VI
Anne Newell

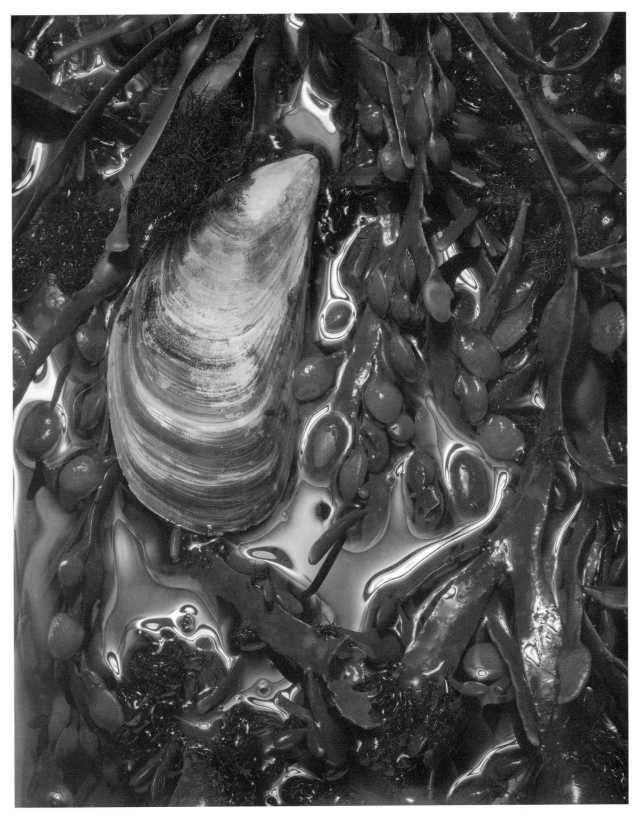

147
Rock pool
Andy Barber

(left) 148 **November**, *David Miller (Surrey)*
(above) 149 **Dawn at the pond**, *Kathleen Harcom*

(left) 150 **Frost**, *Len Perkis*
(above) 151 **Afon Croesor yn y Niwl**, *O Tudur Owen*

152
Insignificance
Edward Gordon

153
Ceunant Coch – Gaeaf (winter)
O Tudur Owen

154
Dŵr a Chraig
O Tudur Owen

155
Monsal Dale
Paul Damen

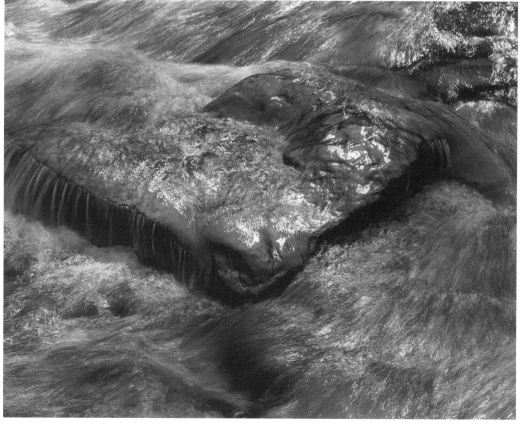

(top left) 156 **Floods**, *Danny Smout*
(bottom left) 157 **Flow #1**, *Steve Terry*
(above) 158 **Retreating tide**, *Peter Clark*

(above) 159 **No title**, *Clive Vincent*
(top right) 160 **Rocks, Hommet**, *Nick Després*
(bottom right) 161 **Fort Hommet**, *Nick Després*

(above) 162 **Dawn, Kennack Sands**, *Clive Vincent*
(top right) 163 **Groynes #1**, *Nick Després*
(bottom right) 164 **Groynes #2**, *Nick Després*

(top) 165 **Pier and slipway**, *Trevor Crone*
(bottom) 166 **South Swale Nature Reserve**, *Trevor Crone*

(top) 167 **End of the road**, *Paul Damen*
(bottom) 168 **Wash sunset**, *Chris Holt*

137

Contributor profiles

Ron Abrahams *(Israel)*
A dental surgeon by profession, Ron has been active in photography for about 12 years. He works solely in monochrome and concentrates on landscapes and outdoor figure work. *(33)*

Daniel Acevedo *(Spain)*
David is a wildlife and landscape photographer from La Rioja, Spain. His work has been published in several wildlife journals and he has also worked with regional newspapers. Having been inspired by the landscapes, David has lived in Ireland on occasion and studied photography at The Burren College of Art in the west of the country. *(127)*

Lesley Aggar *(East Sussex)*
Having recently discovered the surreal landscape of Dungeness, Lesley has returned often to build a series of split toned landscapes, some of which have been recently exhibited in London and at the 1999 Brighton Festival. *(122)*

Ray Anderson *(South Glamorgan)*
Ray began photography 12 years ago as a therapy for stress at work. He joined a local club and quickly achieved his ARPS, with his main interest in monochrome landscape and architecture. His ambition is to get some of his work published so as to share his interest with a wider audience. *(28)*

David Askew *(Devon)*
David began his photographic interest about seven years ago, when with his wife enrolled on a City and Guilds course at Seaton. He has since gained an ARPS in Applied Photography and now intends to concentrate on wildlife and candid shots of working people in their environment. *(125, 126)*

James Austin *(Cambridgeshire)*
James has been a photographer of architecture and fine arts since the mid-sixties. Much of his professional work is in colour, but he finds in black and white the perfect medium to explore the traditional values of the past. *(3, 9)*

Andy Barber *(Devon)*
Andy has been an enthusiastic photographer since being given an Halina 35x camera at the age of twelve. He has experimented with virtually every technique, format and process associated with photography since then, but has found he usually ends up returning to monochrome. Andy is the secretary of Plymouth CC. *(147)*

Neil Bedwell *(Lancashire)*
Neil originally became interested in photography as an aid to painting and drawing. However, a night school class showed him the creative potential of darkroom work, and he now prefers photography as a means of image-making. His aim is to convey atmosphere rather than make detailed records of his subjects. *(116, 118)*

Jim Bennett *(Co Durham)*
Having returned to monochrome photography after trying colour, Jim's main interest over the last few years has been infrared. He is currently the President of the Durham PS and is busy with a Millennium project. *(4)*

Kevin Bridgwood *(Staffordshire)*
Although being involved in photography for some years in the form of colour slide work, Kevin now works for 95% of the time in monochrome. He gained an LRPS in the pictorial section in 1991 and has since had his work published in *Best of Friends* and *Practical Photography*. *(77, 94)*

Carolyn Bross *(USA)*
Her husband's Valentine's Day gift of a camera in 1985 started Carolyn's romance with photography and the path to a new career. Her monochrome images are often selectively hand-coloured to reflect her emotional response to the subject and these have been widely exhibited and published. *(10, 31)*

Alan Brown *(Staffordshire)*
Although only becoming interested in photography in 1988, Alan has had numerous acceptances in national and international salons and holds distinctions of the PAGB and BPE. He is a member of the highly active Moorland Monochrome Group and is currently working to gain enough acceptances in international exhibitions to achieve the recognised honours from FIAP. *(18, 22, 23, 79)*

Alan Brown *(Tyne & Wear)*
Though known to turn his camera to most subjects, Alan's photographic preference is sport, which he feels is too often dismissed as offering little opportunity for creative work. He has been a member of South Shields PS since taking up photography in 1990. *(108)*

Eleanor Brown (USA)
(82)

Michael Calder (Australia)
A Fellow of the Australian Photographic Society, Mike has produced a book of monochrome photographs depicting life at the Tasmanian school at which he teaches. He has also had work published in magazines and this is his third appearance in Best of Friends. (54, 78)

Michael Cant (Essex)
Inspired by the Christmas gift of Best of Friends 3, Michael returned to photography in 1996 after several years away. His future plans include building a portfolio of monochrome pictures taken around Essex churches. (66)

Peter Clark (Staffordshire)
A member of Eyecon and Cannock PS, Peter's passion for monochrome continues unabated with a total emphasis on landscape, for which he was awarded the Fellowship of the RPS in 1992. An avid exhibitor with over 1150 exhibition acceptances, including around 180 awards, Peter holds the EFIAP Silver distinction, is a 4-star mono print exhibitor of the Photographic Society of America and an Honorary Fellow of the Pakistan Salon Group. (64, 145, 158)

Richard Clegg (Cornwall)
Inspired by the high standards set in club photography, Richard gained his Licentiateship of the RPS in 1993 and has had work accepted in national and international exhibitions. His recent move to Cornwall has provided an overwhelming array of potential subjects. (76)

John Clow (Northamptonshire)
John's work has been exhibited widely and published in two Creative Monochrome books, The Mountains of Snowdonia and Snowdonia Revisited. He sees photography as one medium, alongside painting and poetry, through which he seeks to express his feelings. (26)

Gerry Coe (Northern Ireland)
Gerry is a professional portrait photographer working exclusively in monochrome. In his personal work, he works mainly to themes, but takes any subject that excites him. Gerry was awarded the Agfa UK and Ireland Portrait Photographer of the Year in 1998 and in 1999 obtained his Fellowship of the British Institute of Professional Photographers. (61, 83)

Garry Corbett (West Midlands)
Garry has been taking photographs since the age of 10 when he received a Kodak Instamatic as a birthday gift from his uncle Stan. He is a member of Great Barr PS and has had work published in the amateur press as well as Best of Friends. (98)

Trevor Crone (London)
Trevor has had more images published in the Best of Friends series than any other photographer. His work has been exhibited and published widely. He has recently had a personal perspective of Kent published by Creative Monochrome as The Intimate Garden. (75, 165, 166)

Paul Damen (Norfolk)
Paul, who holds a degree in photographic media studies, is an Associate of the BIPP and the RPS and a member of UPP. He is well known as a judge and as a tutor on photography. He has presented two videos on landscape photography techniques. (123, 155, 167)

Sue Davies (Buckinghamshire)
Sue became hooked on photography as a result of enrolling on a City & Guilds modular photography course. Her work, for which she readily acknowledges the influence of John Blakemore, has been widely exhibited. Sue is an Associate of the RPS. (39)

Simon Denison (Shropshire)
Simon is a journalist and magazine editor. In his photography he has been taught by Barry Thornton, John Blakemore and Fay Godwin. He tries to make contemplative work that suggests meanings beyond the obvious, aiming at an ideal of picture-making in which subject and form have equal importance. (48, 114)

Nick Després (Guernsey)
Nick has concentrated on colour slides for the past decade, but has recently rekindled his interest in monochrome, having touched on it briefly when starting photography. He is a Fellow of the RPS and has concentrated on the landscape of his native island. (160, 161, 163, 164)

John Devenport (Kent)
A member of the Mirage Group and Ashford CC, John continues to enjoy exploring the great outdoors with his camera, both for open landscapes and the more intimate details. He has recently gained the Artist distinction of FIAP and is an Associate of the RPS. (113)

Tom Dodd (Gwynedd)
Tom's photographic interest spans some 25 years and is inseparable from his involvement with the outdoor environment. A well known lecturer, exhibitor and judge, Tom gained his FRPS in 1979. He is a member of the London Salon, the Chairman of the Licentiateship panel of the RPS and author of the CM book, Cwm Orthin. (56, 57)

Signe Drevsjø (Norway)
Signe Drevsjø, who favours monochrome photography, has been a serious photographer for the last 30 years.

Signe has taken part in international exhibitions since 1969, gaining many worldwide prizes and the distinction of EFIAP in 1980. *(97)*

Sue Durant *(Somerset)*
Sue has been seriously involved in black and white photography for about seven years and is currently completing her final City & Guilds Photography module before applying for her LRPS. Working as an Art Technician in a comprehensive school, Sue finds time to teach basic monochrome photography techniques to students, thereby keeping alive the traditional techniques of the art and craft of photography. *(8)*

Brian Ebbage *(Norfolk)*
An enthusiastic club photographer for over 20 years, Brian gained the Fellowship of the RPS in 1991 with a portfolio of monochrome landscapes. Enjoying the unreality and atmosphere of black and white, Brian's subject interests include landscape, nudes and infrared photography. *(36)*

Glyn Edmunds *(Hampshire)*
An active photographer for over 10 years, Glyn has accumulated a string of distinctions, including the ARPS, EFIAP and DPAGB. He is a frequent exhibitor in national and international salons and has recently become a feature writer for *Mono* magazine. *(135)*

Roy Elwood *(Tyne & Wear)*
Much of Roy's life centres around photography, especially monochrome - an enduring first love. Although eclectic in choice of subject matter, he prefers to work around themes, currently water, nudes, dancers and the Appleby Horse Fair. A Fellow of the RPS, his work has gained acceptances and awards in exhibitions around the world. Roy is a regular feature writer for *Mono* magazine. *(30)*

Trevor Ermel *(Tyne & Wear)*
A keen photographer for over 30 years and an active member of Whickham PC for most of that time, Trevor regards monochrome as the perfect medium for the 'record' photography he enjoys around his native Tyneside, although he has been known to take the occasional more 'artistic' picture! *(100)*

Hilary Fairclough *(Lancashire)*
Finding it a more expressive medium, Hilary works mainly in monochrome. She likes the challenge of capturing 'that special moment'. The syllabus secretary of Wigan PS, she holds the Licentiateship of the RPS. *(134, 136)*

John Fenn *(Suffolk)*
John returned to photography about 16 years ago and has learned from participation in workshops at Inversnaid Photography Centre. A solicitor by profession, specialising in criminal work, John is convinced that his empty people-less landscapes are a reaction to the people he deals with in the 'day-job'. *(59)*

Andrew Foley *(South Yorkshire)*
Working as a journalist, Andrew has been involved in photography since 1989. He is a member of Mexborough PS and the Chairman of Gamma Photoforum, as well as being an Associate of the RPS. His work has been exhibited in national and international salons. *(32, 87, 90)*

Roger Ford *(Kent)*
Since gaining the Fellowship of the RPS eight years ago, Roger has continued to explore the creative possibilities of the use of monochrome photography. He is a member of Bromley CC and exhibits his work internationally. *(93)*

Trevor Fry *(Essex)*
Trevor has enjoyed photography since the early 1950s and is currently a member of Cambridge & Saffron Walden club. He is a Fellow of the RPS and has had work exhibited in many exhibitions. Although he also works in colour, he retains a real love for black and white, particularly for his favourite subject, people. *(91)*

Joseph George *(Glasgow)*
Joe began taking photography seriously in 1981 when he brought his first slr camera. Printing both in colour and monochrome, Joe finds monochrome a more expressive and enjoyable print medium. Having a photograph selected for *Best of Friends 5* gave Joe "a great boost" and encouraged him to try to get more of his work published. *(13)*

Andrew Gibson *(Lancashire)*
(86)

Edward Gordon *(Surrey)*
Edward took up photography about three years ago and has already achieved a national salon acceptance and the Licentiateship and Associateship of the RPS. He likes to photograph people and wants to spend more time in his native Ireland "before all the travelling people have disappeared or moved to London". *(35, 95, 152)*

Kathleen Harcom *(Hampshire)*
Kathleen's main interest is landscape work, often using infrared film. She has successfully completed a number of courses in photography and has gained the Associateship of the RPS. Kathleen is a member of the Arena and Chimera groups and Southampton CC. Her work has been widely published and exhibited. *(65, 67, 149)*

Brian Harvey (*Wiltshire*)
Brian is a retired scientist who enjoys working in monochrome. He is an Associate of the RPS and a past chairman of his local camera club. His favourite subject is landscape and he has had work accepted in national, and more recently international, exhibitions. *(21, 115)*

Chris Holt (*Norfolk*)
Chris, who is a teacher of science by profession, has been an avid photographer for 20 years, particularly in monochrome but with a keen interest in infrared. He is secretary of the Hunstanton CC and his main subject interest is the "wide empty landscapes of the Norfolk coast in winter". *(120, 168)*

Alfred Hoole (*Lancashire*)
Alfred has been interested in photography since he was 12, and in 1955 he joined Accrington CC (of which he is still a member). He is a regular participant in club, federation and national exhibitions. He takes particular pleasure in landscape and architectural work. *(53, 73)*

Arnold Hubbard (*Tyne & Wear*)
Arnold has been a member of Sunderland PA for over 25 years. His work has been seen in many national and international exhibitions. A Fellow of the RPS and holder of the EFIAP distinction, Arnold is a popular lecturer and regular judge on the club circuit. *(71, 72)*

Fred Hunt (*Australia*)
Fred has been a dedicated monochrome photographer for the past eight years. His major interests have been still life and high key subjects. He was awarded an ARPS in photographic printing last year. *(137)*

Scarlet James (*East Sussex*)
Having only discovered photography fairly recently, Scarlet's work has been shown in various exhibitions including the RPS and The London Salon, as well as having pictures sold both in the UK and in America. *(81, 84)*

Nigel Jarvis (*Surrey*)
Nigel's interest in monochrome photography developed while taking an 'O' level and then an 'A' level at a local education institute. His subject interest is mainly in flowers and landscapes. *(41, 42)*

Mike Kielecher (*Lancashire*)
Mike has been seriously interested in photography for about 25 years, working in both colour and monochrome. He is a member of two local clubs: Bury PS and Oldham CC. His interests are in all aspects of photography, but his forte "seems to be" in portraiture. *(111)*

Filmer Lee (*Perthshire*)
Fil has been snapping madly since the mid 1940s with much success in international exhibitions. Having started with a 620 Brownie Box camera, he used 3.5x2.5 plates and then 35mm film, but has now moved back up to medium format. *(46, 47)*

Trevor Legate (*Sussex*)
An advertising and industrial photographer for over 20 years, he still enjoys the freedom of "doing his own thing" and disappearing into the darkroom with black and white negatives "to be surprised by what comes out". *(27, 37)*

Roy Lewis (*Mid-Glamorgan*)
Regularly lecturing in camera clubs in South Wales and Bristol, Roy has done most of his photography from his car window or in his darkroom. Roy says, "I love taking a few negatives and making up a picture". *(5, 99)*

Barbie Lindsay (*Ipswich*)
Photography for Barbie is not merely a hobby, it is an obsession. Taking pictures, printing, exhibiting and viewing other people's work she says is a "delight". Barbie works in all mediums from simple sun prints, through to transparencies as well as digital imaging. She is an active member of the Ipswich and District PS and exhibits and judges nationally. *(92)*

Graham Lowe (*Cleveland*)
A professional photographer, Graham currently works as a lecturer in photography in NE England. In addition, he undertakes freelance work as well as building up and exhibiting his own increasingly successful catalogue of landscapes and still life work. *(11)*

Jean-Jacques Lucas (*Luxembourg*)
Jean-Jacques specialises in landscape photography and is best known for his series of Icelandic and Scandanavian studies. He has held several exhibitions of his work and has had a portfolio of his work published in *Photo Art International*. *(140, 141, 143)*

Roger Maile (*Surrey*)
The managing director of Creative Monochrome, Roger is sufficiently immodest to select his own work for *Best of Friends*. His main subject interest is photographing people, but he lives in hope of making a worthwhile landscape image one day. He has acted as selector for national and international salons and competitions, as well as judging and lecturing at local camera clubs. *(85)*

Don Maslen (*Gloucestershire*)
(74)

Ian Mellor (*Buckinghamshire*)
A member of the New City PS in Milton Keynes, Ian

enjoys many different aspects of photography, although his main success has been with figure and architectural subjects. Working in monochrome, he was awarded the ARPS and DPAGB in 1998 and is applying for the AFIAP, after 5 years of exhibiting photographs in international exhibitions. *(88)*

Ann Miles *(Cambridgeshire)*
Having been introduced to photography by her father at an early age, Ann is now an active member of Cambridge CC, with her main subject interests being in nature photography. She likes to work in monochrome, especially using infrared film, and has recently begun combining conventional photography with digital imaging techniques. *(14, 15, 121)*

David Miller *(Surrey)*
David became involved in camera clubs a few years ago in order to bolster a photographic interest he shares with his wife. He is currently a member of Woking PS and the RPS. Although he gained his Licentiateship with a mixed print panel, he enjoys the challenge of mono printing and toning most of all. *(148)*

David Miller *(Tyne & Wear)*
Dave says that his reward from working in monochrome comes from the simplifying effect it has on the subject, freeing him to concentrate on the light, form and texture of the image. *(45)*

Peter Motton *(Australia)*
Peter became interested in large format photography while working in the graphic arts industry from 1960 to 1975. Since moving to Tasmania in 1975, when he bought his first 35mm camera, he has spent some years as a technician in print media at the University of Tasmania. He describes the work he now produces as a "reaction to the academic images of the age". *(16)*

Johannes Müller *(Germany)*
Having studied geography, geology and botany, Johannes works freelance in landscape planning, landscape ecology, book publishing and university teaching. He has special interests in the geography of Asia, especially China and the Far East, railway history, rural architecture, landscape ecology and the development of the cultural landscape. *(102)*

Anne Newell *(Cornwall)*
Anne returned to photography after a long period of absence and has thrown herself into the hobby with great vigour, specialising mainly in landscape work. She gained her LRPS in 1993. She has played a major role in organising the popular annual 'day of photography' run by Liskeard CC. *(38, 117, 146)*

Mark Oakland *(Suffolk)*
Mark has only recently taken up monochrome photography and finds both the subject and darkroom work engrossing. He says he is fairly undisciplined about picture taking, although always carries a camera, and finds that most of his opportunities arise whilst at work restoring old buildings and churches. *(124)*

O Tudur Owen *(Gwynedd)*
Since retirement five years ago, Tudur says his darkroom work has improved considerably, spurred on by acceptances in the previous two issues of *Best of Friends*. He is a member of two postal portfolios and of Club Camera Blaenau Ffestiniog (where most meetings are held in Welsh). Most of his photographs are taken in the Welsh mountains within a mile of his home. *(106, 151, 153, 154)*

Len Perkis *(Norway)*
Len's main subject interests are landscape, nature and travel. He has had his images widely published, including use as CM cards, and a major shipping line has used many of his landscapes to decorate its ships. *(109, 132, 150)*

Gary Phillips *(West Midlands)*
Gary's interest in monochrome grew after joining Cannock PS in 1989. He does not specialise in any one subject, having to fit his photography around family and work. He does not enter many exhibitions or chase honours, "happy that my enthusiasm for monochrome is as strong as it was when I saw my first print emerge in the dev' tray". *(34, 55, 89)*

Shirlie Phillips *(Australia)*
A keen photographer for the past six years, Shirlie enjoys all subjects, with her preference for photographing women and expanding her images to mixed media. "I would just like to thank all my friends for their time and patience, therefore allowing me to pursue my passion for photography." *(29, 131)*

John Reed *(North Yorkshire)*
Working exclusively in monochrome for about nine years, John's main interest has been landscape, but over the last few years has been exploring other subjects. Two years ago, John was pleased to achieve his Associateship of the RPS on a project using infrared film in stately home gardens, and has had occasional acceptances in national exhibitions. *(40, 44)*

Peter Rees *(Shropshire)*
A monochrome darkroom entuhsiast for over 30 years, Peter is an Associate of the RPS and former Chairman of the RPS Pictorial Group. John also lectures and exhibits widely and holds the EFIAP distinction. *(6)*

Gareth Rees-Roberts (*Powys*)
Gareth became interested in photography at a young age, helping his father in his darkroom. Working mainly in monochrome, Gareth is fasinated by the graphic possibilities of the winter landscape. He has held numerous local exhibitions and gained the ARPS in 1997. (*69, 70*)

Tom Richardson (*Lancashire*)
Tom has taken a serious interest in photography over the past 11 years, with the landscape as his preferred subject. His work has been accepted for numerous national exhibitions. He is an Associate of the RPS and the holder of a BPE distinction. (*52*)

Mel Ridgers (*East Yorkshire*)
(*20*)

Pauline Rook (*Somerset*)
(*129*)

Richard Ross (*Hertfordshire*)
Richard started monochrome printing in 1987 when he set up a darkroom at home. He now specialises almost exclusively in landscape, working both in color and black and white on 35mm and medium formats. Richard gained his LRPS in 1993 with a panel of toned monochrome prints and is currently working towards an Associateship. (*68*)

Andrew Sanderson (*West Yorkshire*)
After a three year course at Dewsbury and Batley Art College, Andrew worked as a press photograper and black and white printer until going freelance in 1987. Posters of his work have been sold in virtually every country in the world and his work has been acquired almost as extensively for private collections. (*139*)

Hazel Sanderson (*West Yorkshire*)
Using her keen appreciation of lighting, texture, tone and composition, Hazel has the exceptional ability to make a memorable image from a mundane subject. She is also the author of CM's book, *Dales of Yorkshire*. (*58*)

Jim Shipp (*Northumberland*)
After a number of years producing nature slides, Jim now prefers to work in monochrome, but still enjoys and appreciates all forms of photography. (*144*)

Derek Singleton (*Cumbria*)
Derek took up black and white photography in the mid-1950s, and like many at that time, was seduced by colour slides. He returned to monochrome in the early 1980s, specialising in landscape photography. More recently, he has developed a strong feeling for the West Highlands of Scotland, seeking to capture on film the atmosphere of this wild and remote part of the country. (*50, 51, 62*)

Arthur Smith (*Tyne & Wear*)
Having joined Tynemouth PS ten years ago, Arthur enjoys all aspects of photography, especially working in the darkroom and, "waiting for one's latest, hopefully successful, creation to emerge from the final tray". (*104*)

Danny Smout (*Powys*)
Danny has had a keen hobbyist interest in photography for the last eighteen years and having set up his own darkroom, has been shooting exclusively in monochrome. Living in Mid Wales, Danny likes to take landscape and nature pictures. (*156*)

Neil Souch (*Devon*)
An Associate of the RPS, Neil works exclusively in monochrome and his photography mainly features the varied landscape of the west country. He counts himself fortunate to live in area which has an abundance of subject matter to offer to the landscape photographer. Neil's current ambition is to gain his FRPS with a panel of locally inspired monochrome prints. (*119*)

Göran Stenberg (*Sweden*)
A photographic printer by profession, Göran does most of his monochrome printing in his spare time. Using mainly infrared film, he has recently experimented with liquid emulsions on hand-made paper and bromoil printing. (*7*)

Bob Stevenson (*Surrey*)
Bob recalls using his father's Box Brownie in 1938. Since early retirement in 1986, his hobby has become an addicition. He has recently focused his attention on pictorial work and, although he says he has not achieved any real success, he continues to travel hopefully. (*24*)

Nick Stout (*France*)
(*101*)

Brian Taylor (*London*)
Inspired by the works of Alfred Steiglitz, Henri Cartier-Bresson and Don McCullin, Brian uses a 35mm Yashica slr and specialises in printing and toning techiniques. He describes his credo as "30% camera; 70% darkroom". (*103*)

Gill Terry (*Isle of Skye*)
Gill lives on the Isle of Skye where, together with husband Steve, she runs a guesthouse and photo holiday centre. She works mostly in monochrome and is particularly interested in depicting man's influence on the environment, and the influence of the environment on man. (*112*)

Steve Terry (*Isle of Skye*)
Steve is an Associate of the RPS and runs a photographic holiday centre and gallery on the Isle of Skye. He works

in monochrome and colour and particularly enjoys photographing small details in the landscape. He especially enjoys photographing moving water and finds the river of Skye a rich source of material. *(142, 157)*

Alan Thompson *(Surrey)*
Alan has been interested in photography for over 25 years, concentrating mainly on monochrome. He is an Associate of the RPS and has begun to enter national competitions with some success. His current work is based around the process of Lith printing together with the use of various toners. *(1, 49)*

Lisa Thompson *(Australia)*
Having been taken on a school excursion to see a Henri Cartier-Bresson exhibition when she was 17, Lisa was awakened to the art and craft of photography. For the past five years she has taken photography more seriously, having competed at national level with the Australian PS. Her young family is a favourite subject – "sometimes willing!". *(80)*

Rod Thornbury *(Northern Ireland)*
A retired school vice-principal, Rod's interest in photography was sparked as a child whilst watching his father print contacts and, in his teens, seeing his uncle working in bromoil secured his life-long enthusiasm for monochrome photography. Rod has had club and magazine successes and, now retired, is catching up with the negative files he kept adding to in younger years even when without a darkroom. *(60)*

David Thurlow *(West Yorkshire)*
David set up his first darkroom more than 30 years ago and, having lapsed into colour slide photography for a number of years, returned to black and white about 15 years ago. He has recently started mixing his own 'brews'. David says, "I enjoy taking pictures for the sheer pleasure of it – anything that catches my eye". *(105)*

Kirk Toft *(West Yorkshire)*
Facinated by bromoils since he first noticed etching-like illustrations in archival copies of *AP*, Kirk's "love affair" led him into two years of failed experimentation with the process. Six years on brought success and publication of work along with articles related to the process. Kirk is now working in the obscure Oleobrom process. *(12, 96)*

Duncan Unsworth *(Middlesex)*
Ducan taught himself photography about 20 years ago by studying the work of others in books and magazines. Although now working as a television cameraman, Duncan has retained a passion for monochrome still pictures. Having illustrated a number of walking guidebooks, his main subject interests are landscape and architecture. *(2, 63)*

Keith Urro *(Devon)*
Although Keith has been interested in photography all his life, it is only during the last eight years that he has followed the hobby seriously. A City and Guilds course concentrated his interest in monochrome work and Keith now pursues this aspect of photography on Dartmoor where he lives. *(128, 130, 133)*

Clive Vincent *(Cornwall)*
Although starting with colour, Clive is now a confirmed monochrome worker with roughly 15 years' experience of the medium. He tends to specialise in landscapes, primarily of his native Cornwall and his other great love, Dartmoor. A member of Penwith Photo Group, Clive has exhibited his work widely. *(159, 162)*

Peter Waters *(Essex)*
(25)

Emma Weal *(Devon)*
(110)

Simon Welch *(Cambridgeshire)*
Simon has an eclectic range of subjects and works solely in monochrome, with a love for working in the darkroom. *(19)*

Ronald Williams *(Gwynedd)*
Ron took up photography seriously in 1995 following his retirement. He has benefited tremendously by being a member of Caernarfon CC. His interest lies mainly in monochrome work. *(138)*

GLOSSARY OF ABBREVIATIONS

BIPP   British Institute of Professional Photography

BPE   British Photographic Exhibitor – 'crown' awards based on acceptances in recognised national salons

CC   Camera Club

FIAP   (translated as) International Federation of Photographic Art: awards distinctions, including Artist, Excellence and Master, based mainly on acceptances and awards in recognised international salons

PAGB   Photographic Alliance of Great Britain

RPS   The Royal Photographic Society (UK); awards distinctions at Licentiate (LRPS), Associate (ARPS) and Fellowship (FRPS) levels, mainly by assessed submissions of work

UPP   United Photographic Postfolios.